Financial statements:

A simplified easy accounting and business owner guide to understanding and creating financial reports

By

Income Mastery

competence. There are no scenarios in which the publisher or author of this book can be held responsible for any difficulties or damages that may occur to them after making the information presented here.

In addition, the information on the following pages is intended for informational purposes only and should therefore be regarded as universal. As befits its nature, it is presented without warranty with respect to its prolonged validity or provisional quality. The trademarks mentioned are made without written consent and can in no way be considered as sponsorship of the same.

TABLE OF CONTENTS

Chapter 1 - Financial Statements: A Simple Accounting Guide for Business Owners. Learn to understand and create financial reports.

In the field of business it is necessary to have updated financial information to make decisions that take into account the totality of the economic context of a company in question, this way, future actions can be predicted and it is possible to figure out what it is that the business needs to do to prosper in the immediate future and in the long term. When you are your own boss, you need to keep an optimal record of all the operations that can modify the balance of your company, this has its processes and its system, being faithful to the process will allow you to be efficient. Every change during the fiscal period is relevant and must be recorded, so you must learn to do it professionally.

The most important thing for a financial statement is that it is both useful and reliable. In this book we will explore the different types of financial statements according to their objectives and to whom they are addressed. There will be a deconstruction of the concept of *financial state* and we will see what exactly this concept understands and what its real scope is in a business and a given community, since each business directly affects the surrounding economy and, therefore, the society that goes along with it. The company is also being affected by the economic and political reality of its environment.

An average entrepreneur must have a general knowledge of accounting to understand an economic entity in a comprehensive way, in addition, he or she must have the resources to communicate this knowledge and be understood without major problems.

Depending on each country, the components of a financial statement may vary, but in general, they are usually the same, you must know how to distinguish them and make them on your own. It is true that they are usually done by accountants or administrators and you would need one to guide through them, but being said that, you must understand this information to eventually create them on your own and rely less on others during the creation of your business.

All recorded information must be relevant, which can be considered subjective, so you must exercise infallible judgment, as all this has legal implications that can change the fate of your business if you do it incorrectly. The idea is to be accountable to your tax responsibilities and observe your performance, in this way, any other company or person who decides to do business with you and establish an alliance, has the resources to make that decision properly.

So, we want to offer a guide that can be useful for business owners who need to acquire this knowledge and apply it to their small or medium business. This will help you to make decisions regarding the exposed data, evaluate problems to be solved, be conscious about costs, margins, inventory, accounts receivable, expenses or sales. Finally, you can report your profits and generate greater sales, since you will know exactly what you need to do to achieve You can also find alternative ways to improve your business through tax deduction.

Take care of sales, promotions, reduced benefits.

Tangible and intangible services.

Products and services.

Balance Sheet

To start learning about financial statements we must start from the concept of balance sheets. These documents are fundamental for your business, in some countries, such as Colombia, the Financial Statements are known as General Balance, this way we can appreciate the relevance of this document for the assembly of a Financial Statement. However, there are different types of balance sheets and each involves different fields of study.

Generally speaking, a balance sheet has two basic parts: assets and liabilities. Similarly, assets are subdivided into current assets and fixed assets. The fixed asset is the one that represents the assets that the company owns physically. On the other hand, the circulating asset that is the money to receive, to pay, the treasury, in general. Current assets is all equity that is estimated to be spent or paid in the short term, while fixed assets includes equity that should be considered in the long term.

The balance sheet must be a consistent reflection of the company's financial assets and every company listed on the stock market has the obligation to expose its financial statements, at least, the balance sheet, in this way, potential investors can evaluate whether or not to do business with them, in addition to attesting to the legality of the business in question and, for legal purposes, has great value. This report should expose the profit potential and economic position of the business.

Similarly, there are other types of balance sheets, for example, comparative balance sheets that aim to compare different periods of the company's financial position or business in order to analyze the current economic situation and evaluate possible future decisions. On the other hand, the Estimative Balance Sheet, which is created from preliminary information and whose data are subject to future rectifications, depending on how the process unfolds.

It is important to pay attention to how these balances are presented; they must be presented according to the increasing or decreasing order of liquidity in the financial statement. All this depends on which type of assets are presented first, for example, if the assets that have greater liquidity or availability, these are presented first and then the others, in order of importance for the business, it is understood that we are talking about an ascendant order, on the contrary, if fixed assets are presented first and then current assets, we are talking about a descendant method.

Likewise, it is also important to pay detailed attention to the income statement, which are accounting documents that are used to observe the result of a business exercise at a specific moment in time, so you can evaluate the operations carried out, understood losses, sales, profits, surpluses, in this way, we can determine the benefits or disadvantages of some specific operation. The Income Statement is a vital accompaniment to the Balance Sheet, as it reflects the expenses of the company and its level of profits, so we can understand the level of expenses in terms of sales, benefits and services, and assess what actions to take to increase business revenue.

The elements that constitute an Income Statement are the "operating income, operating expenses, operating losses, non-operating expenses, loss before taxes, profit after taxes, legal reserve 10%, profit at the disposal of the partners", among other essential elements of this type of documents, with which we can observe the information that they provide and how they can be very useful for the business. In particular, information on taxes is of great relevance, as many entrepreneurs do not estimate the cost of taxes in the country where they decide to settle. Many people don't consider the expenses involved in paying the tax rate, which can vary, but a good accountant could guide you through the process of settling these accounts, without losing too much money in the process.

Also, the Cash Flow Statement report is very relevant for this type of reports, in fact, they are also part of the obligation of the company when reporting its economic situation, this includes detailed specifications of the activities as collections or cash expenses, thus reflecting the assets of the company and its ability to adapt to changes in socio-political circumstances that surround it, all this in a comprehensive and ethical way so that any interested user can appreciate the data and consider them for future decision making.

All this information is relevant for companies that want to guarantee a long-term return, this means giving security to their partners, investors and potential investors, returning confidence and providing all possible data to ensure honest accounts and future business. Economic stability is the only possible stability in terms of business, having this premise clear will enhance alliances and, likewise, a legal horizon without negative events. If you keep these reports up to date, you will have a complete perspective of your business and you will be able to predict future behaviors and your decision making will be much more real and productive, you will have the resources to know what to do in case of sudden changes in the market and take the necessary contingencies to overcome them.

Some surveys assure that the majority of business owners do not really analyze the Balance Sheets, income statement, and all the reports that are added to them, they only perform them to comply with mandatory regulations and to avoid legal inconveniences, however, they never bother to reflect around them and they operate in the day to day routine and to the unexpected events. This looks like a silly thing to say, if you have the information at your disposal why not use it? This will always be a beneficial complement, it could never harm a business project and, if you are going to do it anyway to meet a standard, the best thing you can do is to make the most of it and use it in your favor. Then, you should consider to take these reports and to use them to consider future managerial decisions, to think long term and to leave the immediacy for the personal life and not for the businesses, your company demands more of you and of the future, if you comply with the regulations to avoid sanctions, it is valid to fulfill them to avoid terrible errors that could cost you your company. A change of mentality can make the difference between success and failure.

Chapter 2.- Products, services and experience.

Let's explore now the concepts that underpin your business and what they provide for a given community. Whenever you start a business you are offering products or services, indeed, but you always have through your experience, all this has a cost to contemplate and involves specific expenses that are reflected in the financial status of your company.

Depending on the nature of your business, your financial statements will have different focus, so the first thing to do is to define what type of business you have and what your business needs are.

Let's start by defining what a product is, a product is any object that can be offered on the market in order to satisfy a desire or need. There are many people who tend to consider that products only comprise tangible products and this is a mistake, there are multiple intangible products such as a travel package or the concert of a particular artist, for example, there is a product that fulfills a function of satisfying a desire or need, is offered to be used, consumed and purchased through a purchase.

On the other hand, services are a type of product, in general, a service is that which can be sold and does not conclude with ownership of something in particular. They are intangible products intended to serve the consumer, a bank or an insurance company are examples of services that throughout history in society have been necessary and fundamental for communities, as are academic services such as schools or universities, repair services, etc. It could be said that many services serve needs rather than desires, yet this remains relative, even if it is a validly substantiated claim.

There is another factor that many ignore in the subject of sales, not only do you get to sell products and services, but you also sell experiences. The experiences of your team, yours, everything you've had to learn to know how to do what you're offering and, the experiences for the consumer, especially when it comes to services. Consumers are not going to buy from a particular place just for the acquisition of something, the business that endures are those who understand that the sale should be more than just a transaction, it should be an experience that dignifies both parties. Sometimes, when a buyer does not agree with the cost of a service, it could be said that the price he is seeing is not just the service, but that he is paying all that it costs (especially in human resources) to materialize such service. For example, educational services, in order for a child to complete his basic and elementary cycle, an enormous teamwork is required, not only of the teachers, but also of the maintenance of the study location, the administrative staff that manages the whole process, even if the child is educated at home, it is not enough with a person who has the knowledge of mathematics and language, it is necessary that this person has dedicated years of his life to receive an education in pedagogy in order to know how to communicate this knowledge in an effective way. All of this has high value and it is part of what you offer in your business.

It is important to define whether your business has an offer of products, services or a mixture of them two. A tangible and pure product would be to sell basic products, toothpaste, hair rinse, soap, detergent, all this is a product that can be sold independently of the service that is intermediary between seller and buyer. On the other hand, there are pure services, such as dental, medical, economic, psychological or psychiatric services. People don't buy these services because they can carry something they say is "theirs" when they go out and buy it because of what those services can provide in an intangible, but substantial way for their long-term lives.

There are also businesses that offer products and services. The value proposal of a company has several components, but it is important to define which is the main one of them, for example, a company that sells cars is rare that only limits itself to sell this product, usually complements this with the insurance service that accompanies the car, as well as the spare parts that might be needed in the future and the maintenance service as well.

In this sense, there are businesses that have a hybrid offer, that is, they offer products and services in equal parts. When your business is a restaurant or a bar, to mention some businesses of this type, people go for the product (the food) and the service you offer is the complement of both what constitutes the offer of the business, in this case, the experience of sitting down to eat in a place with quality food, fresh and well prepared, where they also serve you well, is part of the value proposal. Even if the restaurant has a delivery service and they do not have the infrastructure to allow customers to sit down and eat, it is still a hybrid product where the service is to provide quality food wherever the buyer is located.

In addition, there are services that are complemented by products that serve as a companion. An airline or hotel provides a service that has complementary products, food, shampoo, soaps, beverages, some must be purchased as extra and others are already included in the initial cost of the service. Today, the supply of products and services has become painfully generic. The Internet is supposed to make transactions easier to process, but they have made them impersonal and sterile in most cases. So, focusing your business to be an enjoyable experience will be extremely beneficial for your future and to establish a network of stable customers who always want to buy your products and / or services.

Experience marketing seeks dynamic alternatives to the stagnation of current businesses. According to experts, there are several types of experience that a business has the capacity to offer, sometimes these experiences can be mixed and be several types of experiences in a single offer, anyway, the important thing in any case is that it is memorable for the buyer.

Sensory experiences

This are those that have to do with the aesthetics of the business. To achieve a perspective close to that of the client, we must imagine that we are the consumer and we are observing our business for the first time, this implies that we have to take care of the logo, the colors of the location, how the workers dress, even you as owner, what you communicate visually. We emphasize the visual because the human being is mainly visual, but the rest of the senses are involved in the experience as well, so the communication also influences, the quality of your speech is vital to the sensory experience, what do your networks say, how do they say it? When you enter your business, does it smell like freshly baked cookies? Does it have a particularly seductive smell, or does it smell like nothing? Is there music, do you have a genre that is associated with your business? These are all important questions for your customers to have a satisfying sensory experience, but it is also important for you. Owning a business is not easy, it is a very exhausting commitment, so you have to curate this experience and live it yourself, make it pleasant for all parties involved and take care that the appearance of the business is in tune with the background of it.

Sentimental experiences

Sometimes we underestimate everything that a good purchase can generate in the human being, the emotions of happiness, frustration, fulfillment that arise when someone finally fulfills a desire or a need, when the insurance that has been paying for months finally pays off and eventually saves him from an economic tragedy or when someone buys his first car, that feeling of pride and joy that comes with a transaction. You can make your business a roller coaster of emotions, emphasize the importance of customer service, you can do contests, see what promotions you can do and what products, so that customers feel that buying with you is a bet they have to win.

The experiences of thought or reflective experiences

It is very valuable when an experience gives us pleasure, also when it makes us feel someone special or significant, but we could say that the most important thing is when it makes us think, that an experience penetrates your psyche and makes you reflect or even change your thinking or influence your decision making, is much more valuable, is what all business owners or brand creators should aspire to achieve. Many brands today motivate their customers to think about issues like sustainability, how to make their products green and invite their consumers to be part of the change you want to generate in the world, personalized work done by hand, which values workers and buyers know for sure that what they use is not a product of human exploitation, nor modern slavery, as well as products that are free of animal cruelty, the simple fact that some brands have to mention that they do not participate on animal cruelty, gets you thinking that, the company understands that they are an exception and not part of the status quo. Thus, we will see that challenging your consumers with new ways of thinking, even new alternatives to consume a product they may have been buying for years is a challenge that only experts can afford, but if you have the sensitivity and verbal technique to achieve it, it is possible and much more rewarding.

Experiences of actions

It is associated with thought experiences, because if you change your way of thinking honestly, this will be reflected in your actions and how you live your life. The services and products we consume have a real reach in our lifestyle, this is what is modified with this type of experience. For example, changing traditional delivery methods to an ecological method that goes by bicycle and also has a service according to the laws of work with its workers, will make you see your circumstances differently, you will try to use bicycles more often and mimic this action to other areas of your life in order to have a positive impact on the environment. A good action is a chain of other actions, everything adds up and you will see the satisfaction of improving your lifestyle, all this for a marketing initiative that permeated your life, hence we have to value what we publish on our brand, as it can have a positive or negative impact on our network of contacts and customers. Your brand is your responsibility and communicates a lot about yourself as if it is an extension of you.

Relationship experiences

Again, this type of experiences are an extension of previous experiences, the experience of actions is geared towards individual experiences, but modifying your lifestyle often has an impact on those around you as well, the experiences of relationships are aimed at communities or groups of people, even couples, can be from a romantic dinner to concrete changes in the sustainability of a community, the ecological services of Cabify (a taxi company that fights the market with uber in latin america) are a good example of this. The idea is to put into perspective that an individual never exists by himself without the company of a community that accompanies him, this sometimes is usually small, more familiar, even a couple can be a community. Our actions reflect who we are, and a brand does not exist by itself, it is the reflection of its owner and the community in which it exists.

All of this is relevant because depending on what type of product or service you are proposing, not only must you transform it into a memorable experience for your customers to be able to endure in the market, but you must attend to different things in your account statements depending on what you are offering. When starting a business, many people tend to believe that having a digital business rather than a physical one will save them money, this is true in part, since you also have other types of expenses (minor, certainly) such as where to store products, considering that you do not have to pay rent, you must have a secure deposit, what is the shelf life of the stored product, who runs the networks and promotion, this is a vital human resource for the entrepreneur who is sustained online, so it is important not to skimp when it comes to online promotion.

It is a common mistake to base all your attention on the volume of sales, this can lead to bankruptcy to many businesses, in fact, statistically is what usually happens and one of the reasons is because they are not taking care of the financial statements. Sometimes, with the absurd aim of selling more and more, businesses put significant promotions in place to encourage sales, but this really does not compensate for the initial investment and it was preferable to have the products in stock and break even (i.e., not to lose or gain capital) than to generate loss with aggressive promotions. Therefore, the most important thing is to take care of the profitability of your business and leave the volume of sales as something secondary, this is what will make your business grow in time, not sink, much less cease to exist in the market, think that now we live in a world of high speed and multiple options only a click away, you must make the difference with your offer, but always do it without despair, with a clear mind on what suits you in the long term. Short-term mindset is not effective when it comes to business.

For these reasons it is extremely important that you learn to read financial statements, since they are relevant data obtained through established methods and is objective information, however, is like a book of literature, ie, the language has very clear codes (letters, signs that we understand according to the language we speak) and are translated by the mind when reading them, we all understand what words mean and yet there are millions of interpretations of the same phrase that can lead to diverse actions, so you, as a business owner, must understand these analysis in order to forge your own criteria and not be carried away by the reading of others who may be interpreting the same numbers very differently and take you down a path of imminent indebtedness. See value in your ability to make decisions, it's what will take you far.

Chapter 3: Objectives of the financial statements.

Considering that many people believe that it is not necessary to create exhaustive analysis of the financial statements of a company, in this chapter we are going to develop the reasons to make deep readings of the financial statements and how this can benefit the development of your company or business. To begin with, the most obvious thing is that if, in any way you are going to make the financial statement for compliance only, the best thing is to take advantage of this in your favor, you will not be saving time by omitting it, because the data already exist, is registered and available to you and the rest of the world, do not miss the opportunity to understand how your business can grow and how to avoid the worst-case scenario that, unfortunately, is always in sight when there is money in the equation.

Understanding this type of analysis will allow you, in return, to understand the elements that constitute the economic motivations found in a company, as well as other forms of analysis that are relevant to the development of your business. Not only will you be able to improve your decision making, but you will also be able to describe the measures that you will need to take from the decision making process.

One of the most important things for a business is to establish fixed payments and eventual payments, liquidity and inventory activity, this allows you to understand the exact time periods in which your business has more or less profitability and to what it is due, perhaps in a month you had a significant expense that in the long run will save you more money, then forecast in the long term if this was a successful investment or not. Also, you already have the fixed costs, say, staff and rent (if you have a physical premises) so you have to ensure that every month enters that minimum amount of money to avoid losses that can bring consequences without return. If an extraordinary payment becomes too large, you must weigh whether it is inevitable or if it can be postponed, if it turns out to be inevitable, then you will have to cut some fixed payment as a contingency or look for strategies to have more income to compensate for the expense, you could even prevent this with financial statements and make these strategies with time to cover any eventuality.

One of the most significant reasons for this type of analysis, especially when it comes to small businesses or first-time owners, is the analysis of leverage, this is something that must be estimated in great detail and care, as it preserves the future of your company and your economic stability. To start a business, it often happens that owners get into debt with leverage strategies that will allow that invested capital to be recovered in a given period of time, however, there are many factors that can be seen in a balance sheet that can determine the safety of these gains or the contingency of irremediable losses. Your economy does not have to be jeopardized, all this can be prevented and taken care of in time.

In addition, it is important to think about those people who work with you, everyone involved in your business should know the position that your company maintains with respect to today's competitive market, so they can also prevent any situation that could compromise their income and job stability. Thinking about others is the best way to be stable, as you will have the necessary information from your entire team to make decisions regarding your human and financial resources.

From the information acquired in a financial statement, you can evaluate what resources the business needs and, most importantly, where to look for them and find them to subsequently make the necessary follow-up, in what it is necessary to invest, that is, a company like Apple can live several months, even years, of the products it has in the market, but with technological advances will have to invest heavily in research and development before bringing out something new. Many times Apple (and this can be seen in the Financial Statements that are currently public) invests millions of dollars in research for a product, invests more in that search than in what it costs to create that product, this means that once the research is done, they must ensure that the product is really profitable, the other end of this process is done by many oil or mining companies that consider cheaper to have spills and pay the respective fines than to invest in protocols to avoid them.

You can also consider the benefits and profits of your business, not only what is useful to you as a business owner, but how your business is beneficial to your community or the community where it is located. Sometimes the initial idea of a business is not as profitable as some complements that may arise later, such as, for example, bookstores that are not profitable by themselves, but when they make events and add a bigger cafeteria, the whole concept changes and becomes a profitable business, again we return to the subject of experience, since selling generic products and services can be a long-term problem if that does not become an experience for the consumers of the business.

However, there are several ways to read and interpret the information in the financial statements. The first is the vertical method or historical method, this serves to analyze the economic situation of a company at a given time in time, so we can evaluate the results of certain operations in a specific period. It tends to be plotted and is based on trends, index, percentages and/or financial ratios. On the other hand, in the horizontal method, the last two periods are compared in order to compare budgets and accounting.

Another method of interpreting the financial statements is the trend method, which is also horizontal and takes a specific year as its base and assigns 100% to that year, then determines the trends of the other years in relation to the base year, then divides the balance of the year used as an item and the year used as its base, then the result is multiplied by one hundred and so the percentage of the trend is found. This is important because a balance exceeding 100 indicates that there is an increase between the balance of the base year and the base year, whereas when the result is less than 100 it means that there has been a decrease between the base year and the base year. It is appropriate that the percentages of the trends be compared with other percentages of similar trends, for example, the percentage increase in accounts payable to investors can be compared with the percentage of accounts receivable from customers and then evaluate the profitability of these trends.

It should be noted that it is sometimes impossible to calculate trends with percentages, this happens when in the year considered as a basis there has been a net loss without any profit, just as if at a specific time the balance of the company is at zero, so the calculation is impossible, so this factor must be taken into account when considering methods of interpreting the economic situation of a business.

In another order of ideas, a marked distinction must be made between the analysis of the information and its interpretation. Some accountants do not take into account this difference, it is as if a doctor took a patient's medical history and did not recommend any treatment after reading it. The analysis of financial statements is a job that should not be underestimated in any way, involves many mathematical calculations to establish the integral percentages that constitute the financial ratios and, in general, the situation of the company. However, it is important to note that the numbers that lie in such analyses are sterile signs if the mind does not delve into interpreting them. Interpreting them involves another type of process that seeks to investigate the strengths or weaknesses of the business.

To begin with, we must start with the existing classification of the different types of Financial Statements and what type of information each one includes, so that we can know what you would need them for. First, we can observe the existence of the basic Financial Statements, these include the balance sheet and the profit and loss statement. They are basic because they are considered to be complementary to the total information necessary for a complete and integral analysis of the situation of the company, this is what businesses that need to comply with the regulations that oblige them to publish their financial statements do. This is useful because it allows a company's commitments and debts to be reflected so that investors take them into account in the short term when it comes to investing or not investing money.

There are other types of basic financial statements, such as commercial financial statements, the ultimate purpose of which is to evaluate the closing or contracts for the purchase of goods with credit or external financing. Here you can see the economic-financial situation at a specific date. There are also tax financial statements, which provide relevant information on the taxes that the company must pay to the government, depending on the volume of sales at a specific time. There are also audited financial statements, which focus on companies that are listed on the stock exchange and thus determine their financial instruments, i.e., stocks, bonds, etc. and must be published at the end of each year respectively.

On the other hand, there are also consolidated financial statements, which focus on large companies that are the parent companies of other companies and must consolidate the financial statements of subsidiary companies and establish themselves as a consolidated economic group. Likewise, there are historical financial statements, which present the economic situation of a company omitting the inflationary adjustments caused by the economy of the country in question, this is beneficial for companies that operate in countries with variable economies and have investors outside the country, but in doing this they must also make the financial statement adjusted for the effect of inflation, so you can appreciate the capital of the company and evaluate the result, depending on whether it was positive or negative and how it was affected by such economic adjustments.

Finally, there are the budgeted or pro-forma financial statements, which reflect the time horizon of the company, show the projection that is being proposed for the future and allow to evaluate the budget available for the economic future of the company in a given time frame.

The purpose of interpreting financial statements is to evaluate the viability of one or more projects as long as their profitability is beneficial to the company. Indices or reasons can be determined from the general balances, study the economic impact of a given project, calculate profits, losses and values of an updated value and estimate how much could be earned in the future from it, reflect on the profitability of the project from the calculation of income and expenses of the updated values, among other relevant reasons such as establishing numerical equality depending on the positive or negative results of an action.

On the other hand, there is a method of analysis of financial statements called "The point of equilibrium", created by Professor Walter A. Rautenstrauch, which seeks to present complete information on issues of solvency, stability and productivity. This method is represented by the vertex at which a company's total sales and expenses are presented, specifying the exact moment at which there are no losses or profits for a business, since income is equal to expenses. It is applied from the plan on a project and the profits on your investment. It is the materialization of a company's capacity, since revenues are equal to costs, which is ideal, it is the middle point for an evaluation or, let's say, the zero level, since above it profits are obtained and below it losses are perceived, the tentative costs of production are determined, the numbers of sales required to establish a unit point in sales are determined, the necessary amount is established to raise a new investment in fixed assets and determine the effect that a modification in expenses could have in relation to the sales of a business.

In this sense, the things that can cause a change in the equilibrium point of a company are, for example, price changes in sales, changes in fixed costs, changes in the raw material or in the concretion of the work or the materials used for it, changes in the volume of sales, and so on. In this way, decisions can be made about the profitability of the company, expansion or closure of the same, price changes or promotions to increase sales volume, changes in the human resources of a company, mixing the sale of products if they are related to each other. This method is ideal for companies that sell different products similar to each other, which may have different prices and imply different benefits for the company's overall income, so that decisions can be made taking into account all factors for the company in general, without omitting the specific details of each product or service and its scope for the long-term sustainability of the company. All this requires a minimum acquisition of data, since only the volume of sales, fixed and variable costs, amount of sales and total costs are needed. However, it is important to clarify that this method is not suitable for situations of economic crisis because it assumes that some costs and expenses can be maintained over time and this does not really tend to be so.

Chapter 4: Preparing Cash Flow.

In this chapter we want to delve deeper into the notion of cash flow and its importance for the financial statements and the total understanding of it. The cash flows reflect the values in the cash allocations of the activities or operations carried out by the company. There are different types of activities to consider in this type of report. On the other hand, there are investment activities, which include income generated from the sale of fixed assets, intangible assets or permanent securities, i.e. bonds or shares in the stock exchange, etc. as well as expenses for acquisitions of fixed assets of the same type. There are also financing activities that mean income from loans from the bank or the financial system and expenditure on debts from loans paid off, interest, dividend payments or such payments.

Therefore, for the preparation of a cash flow report, it is necessary to have the basis for the creation of one, which consists of two balance sheets that refer to the beginning and end of the period to which the cash flow statement corresponds, a statement of income for the period in question and complementary notes to the items included in all the aforementioned documents.

However, the process of preparing this type of report must analyze the variations that arise from the comparative balance sheet and thus identify the increases or decreases in each of the items of the balance sheet and conclude with the increase or decrease in total cash. In this sense, it is necessary to determine the cash that has arisen from operating activities, this is basically to translate the benefits that are reflected by separating the items that were not received or that did not imply cash disbursement. Likewise, it is too pertinent not to neglect the rest of the items in order to attend to the cash flow that arose from financing or investment activities, as well as to consider accounting transactions that only involve transfers and do not necessarily imply capital movements. All of this must be carefully considered in these types of statements.

For this there are several preparation methods, there is the direct method, which details the items that have generated an increase or a decrease in cash or cash equivalents, regardless of the currency used, some examples of this are sales collected or any other type of income that has been collected, expenses paid or more income of that quality. This report should explicitly detail the reason for the transactions of these resources in question and expose the items that relate directly to them, this is a great benefit in favor of data exposure, which is always positive when it comes to understanding the economic situation of a company.

On the other hand, the indirect method used to make a specific cash flow report consists of reflecting the data of the ordinary and extraordinary net results of the specific moment that one wants to analyze and to adjust it with all the other items that have influenced the result, but that have not generated income or movements of cash or cash equivalents. The starting point of this method is based on figures that must be adjusted, but that have nothing to do with transactions, nor with the flow of monetary resources, many consider this method as a conciliatory method for this very reason. Therefore, the presentation in this method should be the total result of the period being interpreted and reconciling items.

These reconciling items may be of a type that affects cash and profit, loss or cash in a period other than that analyzed. They may also be exchanged for other items that vary in the aforementioned areas, i.e., that have an increase or decrease in loans due to sales, an increase or decrease in other types of loans, an increase or decrease in assets, an increase or decrease in payables.

In both analysis there are common points, in both there is essential information on the operating activity and its influences on cash and cash equivalents, the difference lies in the changes to be made to the data provided by the balance sheet, they do not reflect the accounts that have not had any transactions, while in the indirect method the changes made, go through the work items and, therefore, the complete information is reflected in the notes.

Depending on the accountant's judgment, the cash flow analysis, whether performed through the direct method or the indirect method, should be disclosed in the complementary information of the Financial Statement, depending on what is most convenient for the company at that particular time. Reconciliation items can be included directly in the supplementary information, if necessary.

It should be noted that interest income must be calculated through the increase in interest receivables or, if necessary, the decrease in interest receivables. Also, it is relevant that the consideration of cash spent on the purchase of goods, either in the period analyzed or in the previous period, which is still in existence in the company. This can be determined by the cost of sales, decrease in inventory, increase in inventory, accounts payable, etc. It could be said that when a company is presenting an increase in its inventory is because it is buying more merchandise than it is selling, then it is necessary to evaluate the sales that must be made to balance these figures to have more profitability.

Finally, it is vital to consider tax expenditures at the end of the year, as this can determine cash flow, so any strategy to lessen this burden is always well received by a business owner.

Conclusion:

It is essential to have a reliable accountant who can guide you in the analysis of the data that is of your interest. It is important that you know how to start interpreting financial statements and that this interpretation is based on the knowledge you have already acquired throughout this book, but also on your experience as a business owner and on the necessary complement of a responsible accompaniment by a professional accountant with considerable and verifiable ethics. As we said before, many people do not properly analyze their financial statements, which has terrible consequences for the economic stability of their business, since it makes them vulnerable to the natural fluctuations of the economy, without any contingency plan or way to prevent them. Similarly, it is true that many times these consequences are generated by total negligence in the lack of correct interpretation of the financial statements or worse, in the incorrect interpretation of them.

There is no point in having a complete financial statement and not taking advantage of the benefits it can bring to the company. A financial statement is much more than the basic balance sheet and income statement. As you have already observed in the content of this book, there are many factors that must be taken into account in order to take full advantage of the existing information in these reports, it is not only unproductive, it is even irresponsible, since there is money and jobs involved. Of course, as a business owner, you should already know all the work involved in raising a small business from scratch, but it is not too much to recognize the work that lies in human capital and that these are the ones who count on you to continue growing with your business.

Likewise, we hope that your business can remain in time and that you can put value beyond the products and services you provide, which are surely of high quality, but today it is necessary that these products and services have the resources to transcend and become a marketing through experience, so that you can have a significant impact on your community, this can also guarantee your permanence in the market that is highly competitive and that is expanding more and more and becoming more generic, so if you manage to differentiate yourself from the rest, while taking advantage of the indisputable usefulness of your financial statements, you will surely have guaranteed long-term success.

Never be fooled by those who say that sales volume is the most important, or worse, the only thing that matters. Surely in your professional career so far, you've already met this type of bosses who only consider this point and precisely for this reason you've made the great decision to start your own business, this is too valid and admirable, go beyond and be careful to be yourself the boss who seeks to sustain a business with sales and more sales, that is no guarantee of profitability.

Understanding how to effectively read your financial statements and why they are so important will make you think differently, and you will understand the real dimension of profitability. Many times, people believe that getting rid of old inventory and asking for more is synonymous with success or cutting edge in sales, this is not so. You have to learn how to develop strategies to have a balance point between your sales and your expenses, evaluate your fixed and variable expenses and be always aware of your accounts payable so that you never have unpleasant surprises that could compromise your business and those who work with you, since, unfortunately, human resources are the first to be affected when it comes to controlling capital damages required for the company to continue operating.

It is clear that undertaking a business is a great responsibility that should not be taken lightly, any business involves expenses that must be considered, even if it is a virtual business and you do not have a physical location to maintain, taking into account the fixed cost of rent or payment installments for the purchase of the premises, likewise the world of virtual sales has fixed expenses that many people do not take into account comprehensively. You would certainly be saving money by starting a business this way, but you have other concerns or, say, issues to address in this regard. If you don't have a place to store your merchandise, you should get a safe warehouse to store it, which also implies a cost that, although it is less than a rent, is comparable to one. So, on the other hand, your online entrepreneurship is a service and not a sale of products, you must have the resources to procure it consistently and, equally, invest in promotion and customer service that characterizes this type of business.

Try to orient your business according to your skills, undertake something you already know, exploit your skills to the maximum, it is true that you do not have to neglect the economic sector and for that there are financial statements, so you have enough data to know all the edges that come out of a business, all this is quite complex and is the basis you need for your business to be really successful. If you are offering a service, product, or better, an enjoyable experience for a community, if you are really satisfying a desire shared by many people or a need that others may not have been able to materialize the way you are, it would be a pity if all that effort were lost by a short perspective on what is reflected in your financial statements. The quality of a business is the tip of the iceberg that hides the economic situation that can destroy or strengthen your business.

In this sense, we should not avoid knowing that, just as we do not neglect a superficial wound when it appears, we do not leave that wound unattended in time based on the premise that it is not a rupture of a bone or something more serious, a superficial wound can become infected and become something more serious if it is not attended to in time. You should never neglect the quality of your business by worrying too much about the financials, so it is important that you have strategic alliances that can take you to the next professional level, surround yourself with people who know what they do and do it well, this is the key to success, delegate the tasks effectively, follow up on them and you will always be up to date. If you manage to have an efficient work team, your responsibility as owner will be much more bearable to the alternative of doing it all yourself, all the time.

In the same way that it is of great importance to establish a reliable and efficient work team, full of people you know and whose work you respect, you must know your clientele. If you know your consumers, you will be able to understand what they need and how to offer it. Have the resources to understand what people need, create a network of customers that is always growing and so, whatever happens, you will have people behind you who will be interested in knowing what you are doing, where and with whom, even if an entrepreneurship does not work, if what you are offering works and has real contact with consumers, they will be attentive to your professional transactions. Many entrepreneurs underestimate the impact they have on their communities and this is as detrimental as negligence in the interpretation of financial statements, everything is closely related and you should never overlook that the most important resource is the human capital and this extends to your consumers, they are the ones who build your business, so put them in value.

Credibility is something that gives money, and this is said very lightly, but just as it is known that time is money, so is trust. If you fail your customers, you are losing money and see it this way, it is really the most effective, it is not a sentimental issue, it is a matter of productivity and profitability, in the end everything falls on profitability and generic services and products that have no human contact, are not profitable at this point of modernity.

In this sense, another pertinent business advice is not to be afraid to materialize your ideas and discard them in time, it is important to understand that the ideas themselves mean nothing and realize them requires courage, have the strengths to see your ideas face to face and sincerely evaluate whether they work in your business plan or not. When there's money on the table, chance and the feeling of attachment to what you wanted to happen doesn't work. You don't have to be afraid to try and fail, that supposed failure will give you the necessary data to know what to do, evaluate risks and take them is not a blind bet, nor a naïve act of faith, of course there are impossible factors to prevent, such as changes in the economy of your country or the political context and its implications in local finances, but those are eventual losses, if you have a margin of potential losses already estimated beforehand, you will know how to take the big leap in the right measure, without the worst scenario being an irreparable loss from which you can't recover. No one regrets being strong enough to open the door to a dream and if your business is your dream, do what you have to do to make it happen.

We hope that the knowledge received from this book will make a difference in your life and your enterprise, surely your future will be full of opportunities for growth, as long as you interpret well the data that the rules of life insist on putting in front of you.